Exploration and Encounters

TEACHERS' NOTES

WORKSHEETS

TWO-CAN

How to Use this Book

Explorations and Encounters at Key Stage 2

Explorations and Encounters 1450 – 1550 is one of the most unusual and stimulating Core Study Units at Key Stage 2 of the National Curriculum for History. The unit explores a major turning point in world history – the first visits of modern Europeans to America, and the meeting of two great and powerful civilizations: Spain and the Aztecs. The topic contains some gripping stories: Columbus's daring voyage into the unknown in 1492, and Cortes' violent conquest of the Aztec Empire twenty years later. The topic offers the opportunity for cross-curricular teaching, linking in well with the Geography, English, Maths and Technology Curriuculums. Many of the themes explored in this Core Study Unit also tie in well with themes suitable for studying over a long period of time as Supplementary Study Units – especially the unit on Ships and Seafarers.

In historical terms, learning about the encounter between Europe and America is valuable because it introduces children to the idea that different people see the same events from different perspectives.

For a Primary teacher, this Study Unit can be both challenging and rewarding: challenging, because much of the material may be unfamiliar; rewarding, since it offers the chance to develop with your class the historical skills outlined in attainment targets two and three of the History Curriculum.

It's specifically with the needs of the hard-pressed Primary teacher in mind that we have produced this book. It is intended both as an introduction to the history of the period (Columbus's voyage to America and the conquest of the Aztec Empire) and as a guide to how to teach the subject in the classroom.

Of course, you won't find all the possible teaching strategies in this book. There are many different ways of exploring the Study Unit with your class – you may discover local exhibitions you could use, or one of the children might even have been to Mexico, for example. But whatever the particular needs or interests of your class, we hope that this book contains plenty of suggestions to get you started on finding out about this fascinating period of history.

Themes for study

This Study Unit falls into two main sections. It begins by looking at Christopher Columbus – why he set out across the Atlantic in 1492, what he hoped to discover, and how he achieved his remarkable voyage from Spain to the Caribbean and back.

The second part of the topic examines the Aztec Empire and its conquest by the Spanish forces led by Hernan Cortes. Children will learn about the main features of Aztec life – food, homes, religion and warfare. They should also look at the reasons why the Spanish were able to defeat the Aztecs, and could round off the topic by an investigation ofthe legacy and the long-term effects of the Spanish conquest, both in Europe and in America.

Activities and assessment

Each section contains suggestions for class activities, ranging from craft and technology 'things to make' to themes for discussion. Along with the activities are guidelines to assessment – which attainment targets an activity covers and pointers to use when assessing what children have learnt. At the head of each section, we have indicated any important cross-curricular links it contains, and these links are also contained within the curriculum matrix on the opposite page.

Books

Along with the guidelines for activities and assessment, each section also contains suggestions for further reading on that particular theme, or for resource books for the activities in that section. Most of the titles listed are easily available and can be found at educational resource centres and schools libraries services.

Curriculum Matrix

	AT 1 Knowledge and Understanding of History	AT 2 Interpretations of History	AT 3 The Use of Historical Sources	Cross-Curricular Links
Introducing Explorations and Encounters		L2–4		
Europe Before the Voyages	L2, L4b, L5c		L3	Geography AT 1
Christopher Columbus and the Enterprise of the Indies		L4	L3	English AT 3
Sailing with Columbus			L1–4	English AT 2, 3
Navigation	L2c			Technology AT 3 Science AT 4 Geography AT 3 Maths AT 1, 4
The Tainos			L3	
The Aztecs of Mexico	L4c		L1, L4	Maths AT 2 Art
Daily Life	L4c			Geography AT 4
Aztec Religion			L1, L3	Art
The Spaniards Arrive in Mexico		L2, L3		English AT1, 3
The Spanish Conquest	L3b, L4b, L5c		L3	English AT 2 Geography AT 1
The Legacy of the Conquest	L4a	L2, L3		
Worksheet 1			L3	Geography AT 1
Worksheet 2			L1–4	English AT 3
Worksheet 3	L4c		L1	
Worksheet 4			L3	Geography AT 1 English AT 2
Worksheet 5	L4c			

Introducing Explorations and Encounters

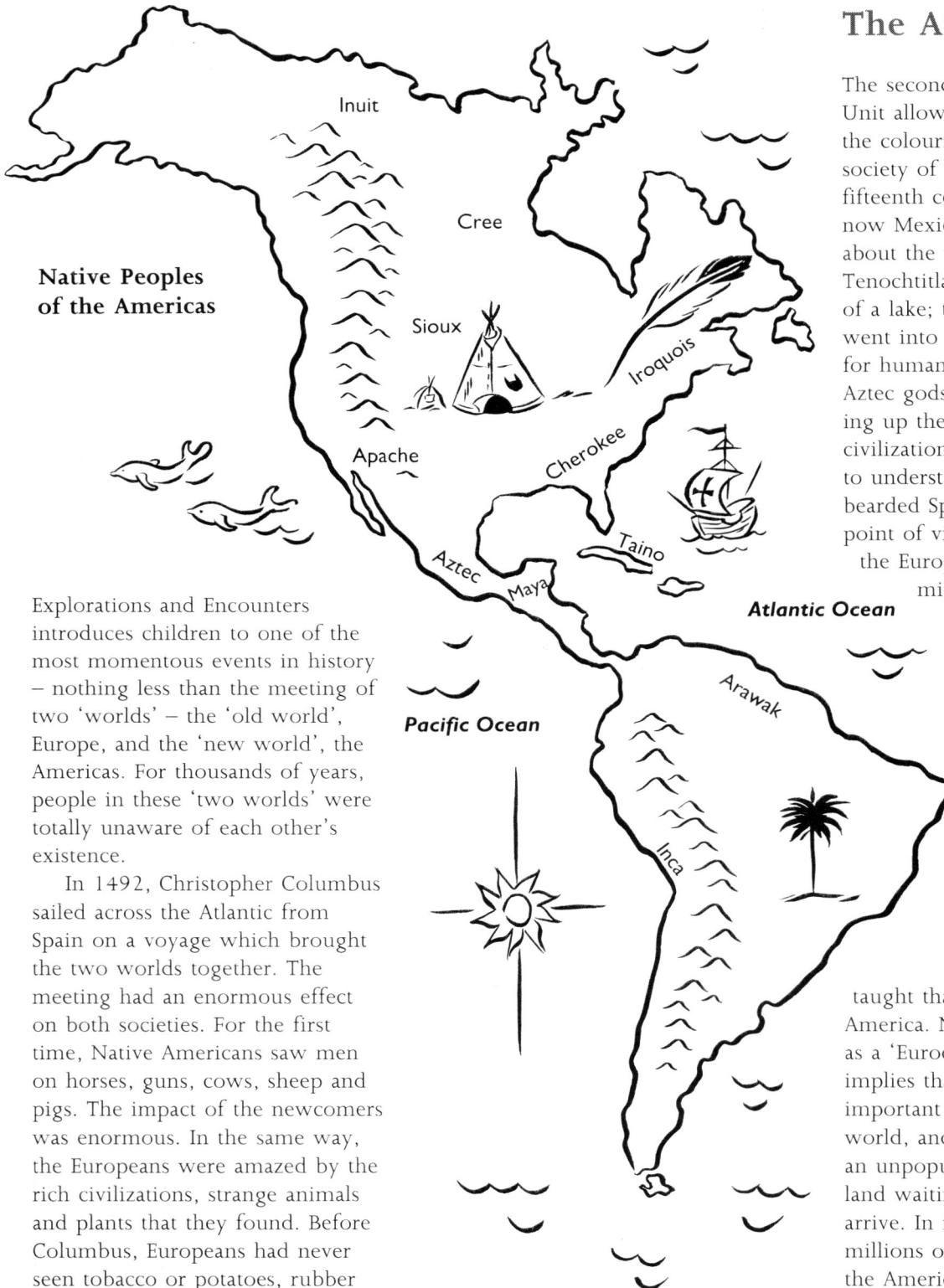

Native Peoples of the Americas

(Map labels: Inuit, Cree, Sioux, Apache, Iroquois, Cherokee, Aztec, Maya, Taino, Arawak, Inca, Atlantic Ocean, Pacific Ocean)

Explorations and Encounters introduces children to one of the most momentous events in history – nothing less than the meeting of two 'worlds' – the 'old world', Europe, and the 'new world', the Americas. For thousands of years, people in these 'two worlds' were totally unaware of each other's existence.

In 1492, Christopher Columbus sailed across the Atlantic from Spain on a voyage which brought the two worlds together. The meeting had an enormous effect on both societies. For the first time, Native Americans saw men on horses, guns, cows, sheep and pigs. The impact of the newcomers was enormous. In the same way, the Europeans were amazed by the rich civilizations, strange animals and plants that they found. Before Columbus, Europeans had never seen tobacco or potatoes, rubber or chocolate.

The Aztecs

The second part of this Core Study Unit allows the children to explore the colourful and fascinating society of the Aztecs who in the fifteenth century lived in what is now Mexico. Children can learn about the vast Aztec home city of Tenochtitlan, built in the middle of a lake; the Aztec warriors who went into battle to take prisoners for human sacrifice; and the many Aztec gods and temples. By building up their knowledge of Aztec civilization, children may begin to understand the arrival of the bearded Spaniards from the Aztec point of view, as well as from the European perspective. How might the Aztecs have felt when they first saw a Spanish ship?

Why 'Encounters'?

Until quite recently, all schoolchildren were taught that Columbus 'discovered' America. Nowadays, this is seen as a 'Eurocentric' viewpoint. It implies that Europe was the only important civilization in the whole world, and that America was simply an unpopulated and undeveloped land waiting for the Europeans to arrive. In fact, there were many millions of people already living in the Americas when Columbus made his first voyage. They had been there for thousands of years, and their 'new world' was really very old. The National Curriculum uses the word 'encounters' rather than discovery because it stresses that children should look at the meeting of the two worlds from the points of view of both civilizations.

Columbus: hero or villain?

'Columbus seems to have been made responsible for everything that's gone wrong in the past 500 years.' Ridley Scott, director of the film '1492, Conquest of Paradise'

Attainment Target 2 of the History Curriculum focuses on how history can be interpreted in different ways. Explorations and Encounters is the perfect topic for meeting the requirements of AT 2.

By learning about Columbus, children will discover that events in the past can be interpreted from very different perspectives.

The year 1992, the five hundredth anniversary of Columbus's voyage, saw a fierce debate over the status of the explorer. It was very different from 1892, when there was a move to make Columbus a saint! In 1992, Columbus was the subject of a mock trial in which he was found guilty of 'slavery, torture, murder, forced labour, kidnapping and robbery'.

In Spain and in America, people argued over how the anniversary of his voyage should be remembered. Government organizations put on official celebrations – Columbus's statue in Barcelona exchanged symbolic rings with the Statue of Liberty in New York. However, many native Americans felt that

such celebrations were wrong.

Teodoro Rasguido, a native Bolivian teenager, was quoted in *The Guardian* newspaper, saying:

'If Spain is going to celebrate 500 years of colonization, a counter celebration should be carried out here. In our land the language, customs and traditional organizations have been maintained during the last 500 years and we are still not beaten. Columbus was responsible for the fact that we are now subordinate to a few people who govern the Bolivian state, who are not Spanish, but mestizos who have both our blood and the blood of the Spanish. The result of the Spanish conquest was the destruction of our culture, an alien language, theft, the Catholic religion, confrontation and the death of our leaders.'

Resources for the study unit
Because this topic has recently aroused much general interest there are a number of good books available for both children and adults on the voyages of Columbus and the civilization of the Aztecs. As you find out more about the topic, you may also want to look at some original sources; we have mentioned some of those that are most readily available (as Penguin Classics, or similar) in the relevant sections of this book. Further options for readers are some of the specially-designed multimedia teaching resources. Among the best is a computer programme package, 'Explorations and Encounters', published by Tressell Publications, Lower Ground Floor, 70 Grand Parade, Brighton BN2 2JA. This package gives children the chance to sail west, like Columbus, facing the dangers of a voyage into the unknown. It also allows them to act as Aztecs or Spaniards, making decisions as events unfold in the conquest of Mexico.

Europe Before the Voyages

Before the fifteenth century, Europeans had not been great travellers and they had only vague ideas about the world beyond their own continent. They were aware that there was a country called 'Cathay', or China, and another called 'Cipangu' or Japan, but people actually knew very little about what these places were like. All the other parts of Asia beyond the Holy Land were called 'The Indies', and Europeans had never visited any part of Africa south of the Sahara Desert.

There were several good reasons for not going far from home in the Middle Ages. Travel overland was slow, difficult and expensive. Sea travel was still very primitive – most ships sailed along close to the coast, and ocean-going voyages were rare and dangerous. Moreover, east of Greece, much of the territory was controlled by Muslim rulers, and most Christians were frightened to go there.

However, for people who were brave enough to journey to the Orient, travel could have huge benefits, and, in the fifteenth century, the Portuguese in particular embarked on voyages of exploration to the south and the east.

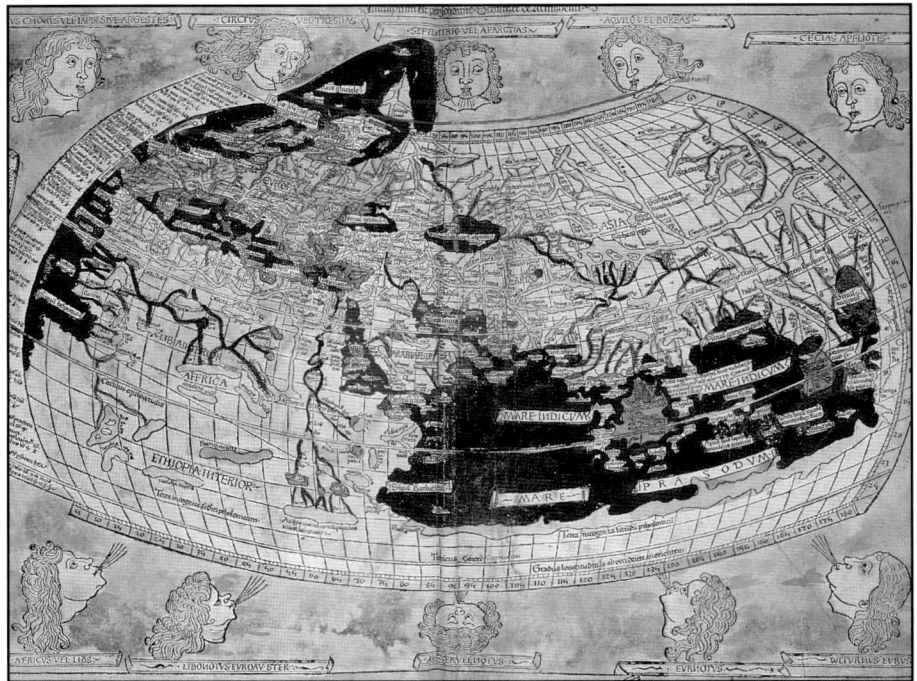

A map of the world, dating from 1486, before Europeans had sailed around the south of Africa or knew that America existed.

Travellers' tales

The few Europeans who did manage to travel in Asia brought back exaggerated accounts of its wealth, mixed up with bizarre stories of the inhabitants. Over the years, these stories were embroidered and embellished even more, until they bore virtually no relation to the truth. One of the most popular books of travellers' tales in the Middle Ages was the *Travels of Sir John Mandeville*, which is full of descriptions of fantastic creatures. This is how Mandeville described some of the people who were supposed to live in the Indies:

'There are many different kinds of people in these isles. In one, there is a race of great stature like giants, foul and horrible to look at. They have one eye only, in the middle of their foreheads. . .'

In their day, these stories were accepted as truth, though we now think that Sir John Mandeville himself never travelled further than the nearest library!

One man who really did travel to the Indies was Marco Polo. He

---

Activity

The simplest way of understanding what fifteenth-century Europeans knew about the world is by looking at their maps. Worksheet 1 contains a map used by Columbus, made in 1489 (just a few years later than the map shown above). Compare the worksheet map with a modern world map or globe, and label some of the countries. Which areas are accurately shown? Make a list of all the places that are missing.

Assessment

Covers **AT 1, Level 2** *Identify differences between past and present times;* **AT 3, Level 3** *Make deductions from historical sources.*
This activity develops basic skills in using an historical source and shows clearly the differences in geographical knowledge between the fifteenth century and today. It is also a valuable exercise in looking at and extracting information from maps (Geography AT 1).

---

spent much of his youth in China, and, on his return to Europe wrote a book describing his voyage. Marco Polo emphasized the great wealth of the Orient, and claimed that Cathay and Cipangu were places where 'palaces were roofed in gold and precious stones were lying around on the ground'. This is how he described Sri Lanka:

'The island produces sapphires and many other precious stones. I assure you that the king of this province possesses the finest ruby that exists in all the world – the finest certainly that was ever seen or is likely to be seen. Let me describe it to you. It is about a palm in length and of the thickness of a man's arm. It is the most brilliant object to behold in all the world, free from any flaw and glowing like fire.'

Spices

Precious stones and metals were not the only kind of wealth that the Indies possessed. Spices were important too. They seem ordinary enough to us today – we see them lined up on supermarket shelves – but in the fifteenth century, spices were worth their weight in gold. They could add variety to a boring diet and, in an age when there were no refrigerators to keep meat fresh, spices disguised the taste of dried, salted or rotting meat.

Most spices are the seeds and bark of plants which grow in hot countries, such as India, Sri Lanka and the Moluccas. They had to travel a long way before they reached the kitchens of Europe, and they became more expensive the further they travelled. Muslim merchants brought them by sea from India to Egypt, where they were sold at a profit to Italians, who in turn made a profit by selling them to the rest of Europe. By the fifteenth century, other Europeans were realizing that if they sailed directly to the lands where spices grew, they would not have to pay such high prices. Anyone who made such a voyage would become rich and famous.

Discussion
Bring in some spices for the class to look at: peppercorns, cloves, cinnamon, coriander and cumin seeds. Grind them up and let the children sniff them (apart from the pepper!) Discuss the strong and fragrant smells, and explain why they were popular. Then go on to talk about the wider reasons that Europeans went on voyages of discovery in the fifteenth century. Make a list of all the other commodities besides spices that they hoped to bring home from the East.

Assessment
Covers **AT 1, Level 4b** *Show an awareness that historical events usually have more than one cause;* **AT 1, Level 5c** *Show how different features in an historical situation relate to each other.* The reasons behind the voyages of discovery are complex and interlinked, so it may be best to discuss them as a class with fairly clear teacher direction.

Books
For a closer look at The Travels of Marco Polo and The Travels of Sir John Mandeville, the original books are both available as Penguin Classics. For children, The Travels of Marco Polo (Richard Humble, Franklin Watts, 1990) is good on Europe before the voyages of discovery.

Christopher Columbus and the 'Enterprise of the Indies'

In the 1400s, the countries of Europe began to look for new sea routes to the riches of the Indies. The first people to set off were the Portuguese. They sailed south down the coast of Africa, and finally rounded the Cape of Good Hope in 1488.

One of the many seafarers who served the king of Portugal was an Italian called Christopher Columbus. Born in the year 1451,

Columbus came from a fairly humble background (his father was a weaver), but he went to sea as a boy and quickly became an experienced and respected sailor. His voyages took him across virtually the whole of the known world, from Greece to Madeira and as far north as Iceland. As a merchant seaman in Portugal, Columbus conceived a daring plan to find a new route to Asia.

Columbus's plan

Columbus's plan was to reach the east (Japan and China) by sailing west, across the unknown Atlantic Ocean. The best way to explain this plan to your class is with a globe. You can show that if you keep travelling west from Spain you do eventually reach Japan.

In an age when most ships rarely left the sight of land for long, this was a very brave idea. All educated people knew that the world was round, but no one knew whether it was possible for a ship to sail right across the Atlantic. There were many superstitions about the ocean, and it was believed to be a place of darkness and storms.

Columbus himself thought it was possible to sail across the Atlantic, but only because he made a big mistake – he thought that the world was much smaller than it really is. He drew a map showing Japan just a short sailing distance from Europe. Luckily for Columbus, the Caribbean islands lay in his path, just where he expected to find Japan.

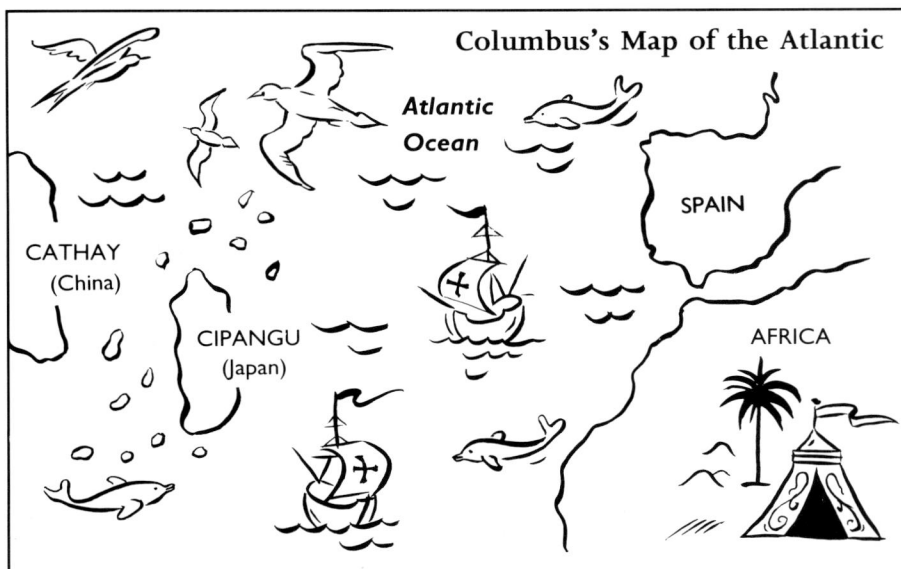

Columbus's Map of the Atlantic

Atlantic Ocean

SPAIN

CATHAY (China)

CIPANGU (Japan)

AFRICA

Books
There are several good children's books that tell the story of Columbus and his voyage: The Voyages of Columbus (Richard Humble, Franklin Watts, 1990); Christopher Columbus (Ken Hills, Kingfisher, 1991); Westward with Columbus (John Dyson and Peter Christopher, Hodder and Stoughton/ Madison Press, 1991). Explorer (Rupert Matthews, Dorling Kindersley, 1991) is a beautifully produced book on all the explorers. Columbus: The Triumphant Failure (O Postgate and N Linell, Kingfisher, 1991) has a useful concluding section on the character and motives of the explorer. To look more closely at Columbus's character, you could also try The Four Voyages of Christopher Columbus (J M Cohen, Penguin), a collection of primary sources, which includes Columbus's log books and his letters to Ferdinand and Isabella.

Christianity and fighting Islam. In 1492, they completed the Christian reconquest of Spain, and drove the last Muslims into North Africa. At the same time, they forced all the Jews in Spain to become Christians or to leave the country.

Columbus's plan appealed to Ferdinand and Isabella's crusading ambitions. It offered a chance to spread the Christian religion in distant lands, while the wealth that Columbus would bring back from the Orient could be used in the war against the Muslims.

Searching for a sponsor

Columbus spent eight years trying to get the rulers of western Europe to sponsor, or back, his voyage. He had to convince them that his plan had a good chance of succeeding, but he was not helped by the demands he made. He wanted to be given the title 'Admiral of the Ocean Sea', to be

Viceroy of all the countries he discovered and to receive a tenth of all the treasure he found. For a poor foreigner from a humble background, these were very big demands. The king of Portugal refused to support him, and his plans were also turned down by the English. At last, in 1492, he won the support of the Spanish monarchs, Ferdinand and Isabella.

The Spanish monarchs were crusaders, dedicated to spreading

Setting sail

Columbus finally set out from southern Spain in August 1492. He had just three ships: the *Santa Maria*, the *Pinta* and the *Nina*. Compared with the ocean-going ships of today, these vessels seem tiny. The *Santa Maria* was the largest, but even it measured no more than 30 metres long. It had a large mainsail, and three or four smaller sails.

Discussion

Columbus is said to have had three main motives for wanting to go to the Indies: God, gold and glory. God, because he wanted to take the Christian religion to the Indies; gold because he wanted to be rich, and glory, because he came from a humble background and wanted to be acknowledged as a famous and important person. In fact no one can be completely sure exactly what kind of a man Columbus was. Different historians attach importance to different motives so that Columbus has been painted as both a genius with a vision and a self-seeking opportunist.

With your class, talk about what kind of a man Columbus might have been. What different words can you find that might describe him? Brave? Stubborn? Greedy?

Activity

Now ask the children to pretend that they are Columbus. They must write a letter to the king and queen of Spain, asking them for money and describing all the benefits that will result from the voyage. (If you have already made a list of general reasons behind the voyages of discovery, the children will probably find it helpful to refer to that.)

Assessment

Covers **AT 3, Level 3** *Make deductions from historical sources.* This activity encourages children to work out what Columbus's (and Ferdinand and Isabella's) motives would have been, starting from the basic facts of what actually happened. In discussion, more able children may be able to understand that, although we know what Columbus did, we do not have enough evidence for anyone to be sure exactly why he did it. (**AT 2, Level 4** *Show an understanding that deficiencies in evidence may lead to different interpretations of the past.*)

Sailing with Columbus

Coumbus's voyage allows you to discuss life at sea with your class. What was it like being stuck in a tiny wooden ship for weeks on end? What did the sailors do? How did they feel? What were the smells and sounds of the sea?

Life on board

We would have found life on board one of Columbus's ships very uncomfortable indeed. The men had to do without many of the things we take for granted every day. They had no beds or baths, for example. They slept out on the open deck, and, if they washed at all, they used sea water. They hardly ever changed their clothes and they let their beards grow. There were no toilets, so the sailors went over the side of the ship, or, if the weather was rough, in the bottom of the hold. The smell below decks was usually horrible after a few days at sea!

Food was boring and limited. The staples were ship's biscuit (a kind of hard, dry bread), dried fish and salted meat. If the weather was fine, the sailors would have one hot meal a day, cooked in a special metal tray filled with sand on which the ship's boys built a fire. But when it rained there would be no hot food at all.

This sort of food must have made the sailors very thirsty, yet all they had to drink was vinegary wine and the small amount of fresh water that the ship could carry. After a few days at sea, even this water would have been stale and tasted disgusting.

Not surprisingly, life on board ship carried all the health risks of a bad diet and filthy conditions. Many sailors suffered from dysentry and 'ship's fevers'. Since they ate no fresh fruit and vegetables, scurvy, which is caused by a lack of vitamin C, was common too.

The poor conditions of life at sea were contrasted vividly with the pleasures of land travel by a Spaniard called Eugenio de Salazar:

'How pleasant it is to travel on land, well mounted and with money in your purse. You meet all kinds of people along the way. If today you are forced to stay in some poor village where the food is scanty and bad, tomorrow you may be in an hospitable and well-provided city.

But at sea there is no hope that the road, or the host or the lodging will improve. Everything grows steadily worse; the ship struggles more and more and the food gets scantier and nastier every day.'

Activity

Worksheet 5 is a cross-section of Coumbus's flagship, the *Santa Maria*. Ask the children to add to the cross-section by drawing in Columbus and the members of the crew, showing and labelling all the various activities. They could also load the hold of the ship with all the different supplies it needed. There should be someone on lookout, a helmsman holding the tiller and an officer in charge. Some sailors might be scrubbing the decks or baling water out of the hold while others rest, playing at dice or perhaps fishing. You could even show someone being seasick!

You might wish to enlarge the worksheet when you photocopy it, to give the children more space for their drawings.

Assessment

Covers **AT 1, Level 4c** *Describe features of an historical period.* By completing the worksheet, children are developing an understanding of Columbus's ship and how it was used. (If children find realistic pictures hard to draw, stick figures are just as effective.)

What did the sailors do?

The sailors were divided into two groups, or watches. One watch looked after the ship for four hours while the other watch rested. The officer in charge kept a careful eye on the weather in case the wind direction changed. He gave orders to the helmsman, who steered the ship, and to the sailors, who altered the way the sails were set. The men chanted songs as they pulled at the ropes which raised the sails.

The sailors also had to scrub the decks with sea water and make repairs. Each morning, they went down to the hold to pump out any water which had seeped through the wooden sides of the ship.

Fears

Besides the discomfort and monotony of the voyage, sailors also suffered from fear. Everyone's life depended on the weather: if the wind did not blow, the ship would be stranded far from land; if it blew too strongly, the ship could be wrecked. Columbus's crew's greatest fear was that they would not find land, and would have to keep sailing until their supplies ran out.

The men were all very religious, and at regular intervals during the day the youngest boys on each ship would lead prayers. At nightfall they said a special Latin prayer, called the 'Salve Regina', to the Virgin Mary.

Signs of land

The sailors spent much of the time looking for signs of land. They used lines weighted with lead, dropped over the side to test the depth of the water. This told them whether the sea-bed was starting to slope up towards a coast. They also watched the sea for floating twigs and the sky for birds. Both might indicate land. Land birds, for example, flap their wings much more than sea birds, which tend to glide. If the sailors spotted a bird flapping its wings, it was a good sign of approaching land.

Navigation

Columbus's greatest challenge was navigation, and the National Curriculum requires children to learn about the technical problems which he faced. How did he find his way out on the open sea, with no maps or landmarks? Earlier Portuguese explorers had simply followed the coastlines of Europe and Africa, but Columbus was sailing into an empty expanse of unknown water. There are various navigational methods which he used and which you can find out about. They all involve some good science, geography and maths activities.

Dead reckoning

The most straightforward way of navigating was dead reckoning. Throughout the day, the sailors had to work out the speed of the ship and the direction in which it was sailing, and then mark out their course on a sheepskin chart.

Speed was measured by dropping chips of wood over the side at the front of the ship and seeing how quickly the ship passed them by; direction was worked out with a magnetic compass.

Each ship also had a large sandglass, like an egg timer, which was used to keep track of the time of day. The sand took half an hour to pour through, and then it would be turned over by the ship's boy. He constantly had to keep a close eye on the glass.

Dead reckoning can tell you how far you have travelled in relation to your starting point, but to be at all accurate, it does require great skill. The navigator had to bear in mind any changes in the winds and currents which would blow the ship off its course.

Activity
Make a sandglass

You will need: two plastic bottles; dry sand or washing powder; sticky tape; a sharp craft knife.

● Cut the top and bottom off each of the plastic bottles, and throw away the middle sections.

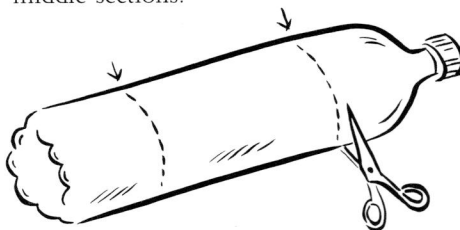

● Tape the top and bottom of each bottle back together again.

● Tape the two bottle lids together as shown. With a darning needle, prick a large hole through them.

The quadrant

● Screw the lids onto the top of the first bottle.

● Pour sand into the second bottle.

● Screw the first bottle into the second bottle.

● Turn the bottles upside down so that the sand runs through.

Time how long the sand takes to run through from one bottle to another. Can the children work out how much sand they will need for the sandglass to time exactly one minute?

Assessment
Covers **AT 1, Level 2c** *Identify differences between past and present times.* This simple activity explains one way in which time was measured before clocks and watches became common. It is also a good exercise in estimating amounts and applying simple maths (Level 3 of Maths AT 1, *Using and applying mathematics*).

Navigators also used an instrument called a quadrant, which could measure the height of the Pole Star in the sky. The Pole Star was important because it appears to stay in the same place while the other stars revolve around it. The further north you travel, the higher in the sky this star appears. If you travel south, it gets lower and lower and eventually disappears. As a result, you can work out how far north or south you have travelled by measuring the height of the star.

Columbus believed that he would reach Japan by sailing due west from the Canaries. By using a quadrant, he could check that he had not wandered off course to the north or the south.

Prevailing winds

Columbus was helped by the system of prevailing winds. Throughout the world's oceans, the wind tends to blow in a set pattern. In the North Atlantic, this pattern is a vast circle with an area of calm in the centre. Anyone who understands this pattern can use it to carry their ship forward. Sailors who did not know about the winds could easily end up becalmed, or with the wind against them. This would have been the fate of Columbus if he had tried sailing due west from Spain.

Columbus actually sailed south to the Canary Islands before heading west, making use of the prevailing wind pattern. He may well have known about the prevailing winds before he set off on his voyage; the Portuguese were already building up a great deal of knowledge about Atlantic winds. Or he might just have been lucky, bcause he believed that he would find Japan due west of the Canaries.

Whatever the case, Columbus found the route across the Atlantic and back which would be used by all future sailing ships.

Cross-Curriculuar Links:
Technology AT 3
Planning and making
Science AT 4
Physical processes
Geography AT 3
Physical geography
Maths AT 1 Using and applying maths; **AT 4** Shape and space

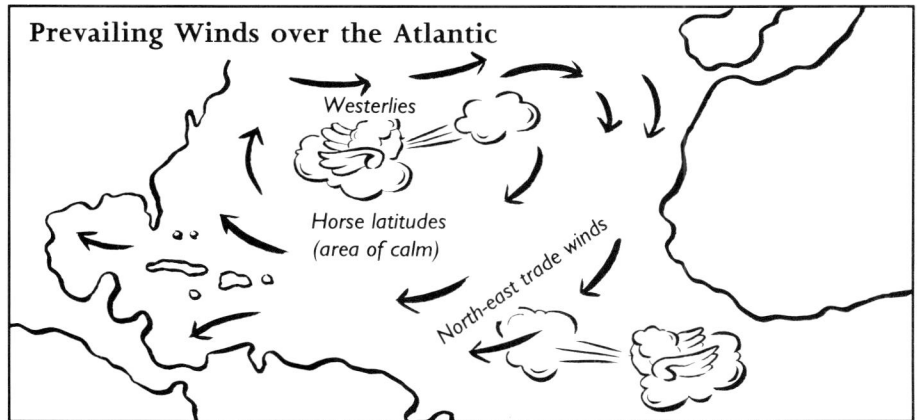

Prevailing Winds over the Atlantic

Westerlies

Horse latitudes (area of calm)

North-east trade winds

Activity
Make a quadrant

You can make your own simple quadrant and use it to measure the angle between yourself and any distant raised point. You will need: a piece of thick card; a length of string; a straw; a lump of Plasticine; sticky tape.

● Cut the card into one quarter of a circle.

● With a protractor, measure out 90 degrees around the curved edge of the piece of card.

● Fix a drinking straw along on one of the straight edges with sticky tape.

● Tape one end of the length of string to the corner of the card. Weight the other end of the string with Plasticine.

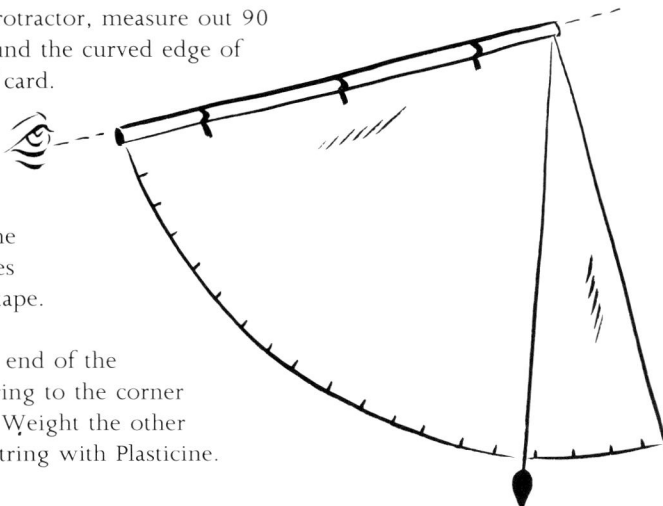

Look through the straw at the point you want to measure, and read off the angle where the string falls across the quadrant's curved edge. (In Columbus's day, this curved edge was often marked with the names of all the major ports in Europe and Africa. By pointing the quadrant towards the Pole Star, the navigator could see whether he was in the same latitude as his home port, for example.)

Assessment
Covers **AT 1, Level 2c** *Identify differences between past and present times.* Rather like the sand-glass, this simple quadrant shows a fifteenth-century solution to a difficult technological problem. However, the maths involved (measuring in degrees) is more complicated, and covers Level 5 of Maths AT 4, *Shape and Space.*

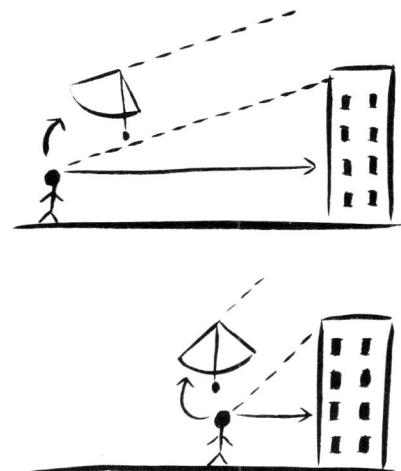

The Tainos

On 12 October 1492, Columbus finally landed on a tiny Caribbean island, inhabited by naked, brown-skinned people. Today, we call these people Tainos or Arawaks – you will find both names in books. Columbus himself called them 'Indians' because he thought he had reached the Indies.

In his captain's log, Columbus wrote a famous entry, describing the Tainos. This description tells us a great deal about his attitude to foreign peoples:

'They do not carry weapons or know of them, for I showed them swords and they took them by the blade and cut themselves through ignorance . . . They should be good and clever servants, since they quickly repeat anything that is said to them. I believe they would easily be made Christians, as it seemed to me they had no religion.'

The Tainos lived in round huts made from canes and thatched with palm leaves. Inside the huts, they slept in cotton hammocks, tied to the central pole. They grew maize and cassava, hunted with bows and arrows, and fished from canoes made from hollowed out tree trunks. To the Spaniards, the strangest thing about the Tainos was that they smoked the rolled up leaves of a plant called tobacco.

Discussion

With your class read out this passage from a letter written by Columbus to Ferdinand and Isabella of Spain:

'As soon as I came to the Indies I seized some natives . . . These men soon understood us, and we them, either by speech or signs. I still have them with me and, despite all the conversation they have had with me, they are still of the opinion that I come from the sky and have been the first to proclaim this wherever I have gone. Then others have gone running from house to house shouting: "Come and see the people from the sky!"'

The Tainos had no idea that Columbus had travelled from a distant land. They did not know that distant lands existed and they had never seen anything as big or strangely built as the Spanish ships. As far as the Tainos were concerned, Columbus was so alien that he might just as well have arrived in a flying saucer.

How would it have felt to be a Taino? Ask the children to imagine that they are Tainos – can they think of all the strange and new objects that the Spanish brought with them? They could draw pictures of these objects.

Assessment

Covers **AT 3, Level 3** *Make deductions from historical sources.* Using the information available to us, can children understand the Tainos' encounter with Columbus from the Tainos' point of view?

Books

Christopher Columbus (John D Clare, Bodley Head, 1992) contains a useful section on the Tainos.

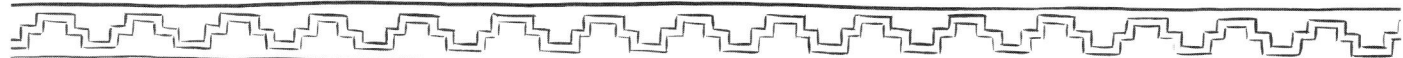

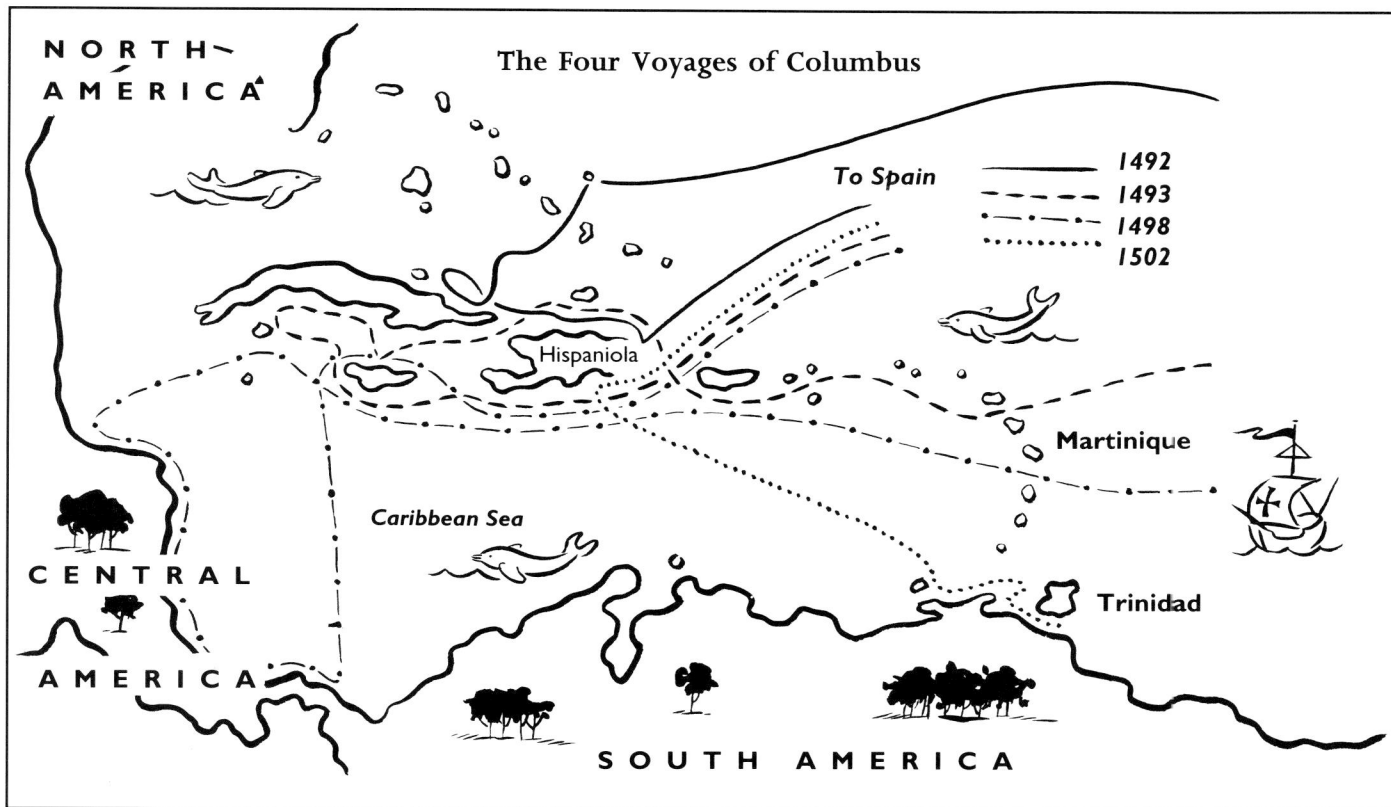

The Four Voyages of Columbus

NORTH AMERICA

To Spain

—————— 1492
– – – – – 1493
·–·–·–· 1498
············ 1502

Hispaniola

Martinique

Caribbean Sea

Trinidad

CENTRAL AMERICA

SOUTH AMERICA

How do we know?

Today, there are no Tainos left on the islands visited by Columbus. To find out what they were like, we rely on what the Spaniards wrote about them and on archaeology. Columbus himself noticed that the Tainos had very broad foreheads, and Taino skulls found by archaeologists show that the Tainos must have produced this effect deliberately, by compressing the heads of babies. Archaeologists have also found carvings and pottery figures. These are thought to be 'zemis', spirits or ancestors who protected the Tainos. The people kept them in their huts and offered food to them.

Hispaniola

During the winter of 1492–93, Columbus sailed around the Caribbean, looking for signs of gold. On one island, Haiti, he noticed Tainos wearing gold nose ornaments and decided to leave a number of sailors there to found a small Spanish settlement. It was named Hispaniola.

Columbus then returned to Spain, taking with him some of the Tainos and examples of the plants and animals he had found in the Caribbean. At the court of Ferdinand and Isabella, he was greeted as a great hero. However, Columbus greatly exaggerated the wealth of Hispaniola: ' Hispaniola is a wonder', he claimed. 'There are many great rivers with broad channels and the majority contain gold . . . In Hispaniola there are many spices and large mines of gold and other metals.'

Because of Columbus's exaggerated descriptions, 1,200 Spanish settlers returned to Hispaniola with him the following year, all hoping to become rich quickly. They were disappointed, and although the Tainos were forced to mine for gold it was soon clear that there were hardly any precious metals on the island. Over the next five years, the colony was unruly and discontented, and the Tainos rebelled against the Spanish. In 1500, Ferdinand and Isabella decided to send a Spanish nobleman to rule Hispaniola.

Within just fifty years, the Taino population had disappeared, wiped out by overwork, European diseases or Spanish swords. In their place, African slaves began to be shipped to the Caribbean.

Columbus himself made two more voyages to the New World and explored many of the islands of the Caribbean. He also visted what is now Venezuela and sailed along the western coast of Central America. However, when he died at the age of fifty-three in 1506, he still believed that he had discovered the route to the Indies. Europeans only slowly began to realize just what the New World was, and exactly how many riches it contained.

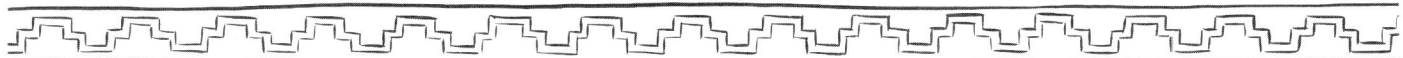

The Aztecs of Mexico

It was not until they began to explore the interior of Central America that the Spanish settlers in the Caribbean found the gold and riches they were looking for. They also found the Aztecs – the subject of the second part of this study unit.

The Aztecs were one of the native peoples of Central America, and they controlled a large area of land in what is now Mexico. Although we talk about the Aztec 'empire', in fact, the Aztecs themselves lived in quite a small area of central Mexico, on and around lake Texcoco, and they did not rule all the other peoples of their empire directly. Instead, they demanded regular payments of 'tribute' – jade and precious feathers, animal skins, foodstuffs and slaves. This tribute provided the Aztecs with food and luxury items that they could not produce for themselves.

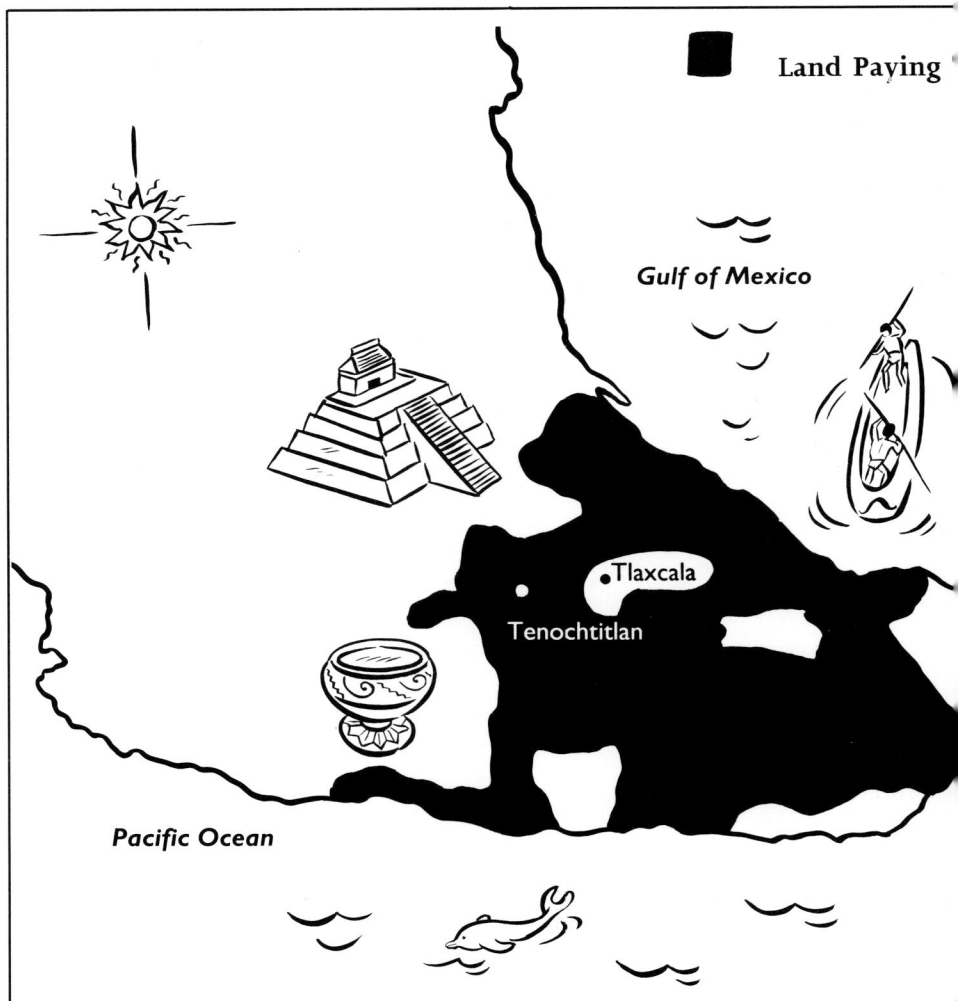

Land Paying

Gulf of Mexico

•Tlaxcala

Tenochtitlan

Pacific Ocean

Activity
Worksheet 3 shows how the Aztecs used pictograms to record all the amounts of tribute that conquered peoples had to pay them.

Assessment
Covers **AT 1, Level 4c** *Describe different features of an historical period;* **AT 3, Level 1** *Communicate information from an historical source.* By working out the tribute puzzles, children are developing historical knowledge of a fairly complex feature of Aztec life, while making use of an historical source (the information about Aztec tribute) at a simple level. This activity is also an introduction to understanding place values in whole numbers (Maths AT 2, Level 4).

Warfare

For most of the time, the peoples of Mexico were left to run their own affairs as long as they paid tribute to the Aztecs. If they failed to pay, they would be attacked by Aztec warriors.

The Aztecs were often at war, but they fought a very ritualistic type of warfare. The aim was not to kill the enemies in battle, but to take them prisoner so they could be sacrificed later to the Aztec gods. The warriors gained social status through capturing prisoners; only successful warriors were allowed to wear fine clothes and jewellery.

... to the Aztecs, 1519

Maya

For protection in battle, the Aztecs wore padded body suits, rather like long johns. They were armed with swords and spears, which were edged with blades made from obsidian (a clear, hard, volcanic stone similar to glass). Their shields and head-dresses were decorated with feathers. Captains had colourful banners strapped to their backs so that their men could see them on the battlefield. There were also special warrior orders, who dressed as jaguars or eagles. An entire Aztec army must have looked terrifying on the battlefield.

Montezuma

The Aztec ruler was a man called Motecuhzoma, which means 'Angry Lord'. His name is usually simplified to Montezuma or Moctezuma. (You will find both versions in children's books.) The Aztecs treated him almost as a god; people were not allowed to look him in the face.

Montezuma wore a beautiful head-dress made from the green feathers of the quetzal bird. The children can make their own version of this out of paper.

You will need: cardboard; green paper (crepe paper or card will do); scissors; a stapler; gold paper and coloured pens.

● Cut out a strip of plain card, long enough to fit around a child's head, and shaped with a larger 'bump' at the front to provide support for the feathers.

● Try the strip of card for size by winding it around someone's head, and then staple the ends together so that it can be worn as a head-band.

● Cut out the green paper into long feather shapes. Staple or glue them to the front of the head-band. Put a few longer feathers in the middle.

● Montezuma's head-dress was also decorated with small pieces of gold, shaped like half-moons. You could get the same effect with gold paper or pens.

Activity

Ask the children to draw some pictures of Aztec warriors going into battle and label their weapons and equipment. Children could use the information you have discussed in class, the head-dress they have made, and any information they can find in books about the Aztecs.

Assessment

Covers **AT 1, Level 4c** *Describe features of an historical period.*
AT 3, Level 4 *Put together information from different historical sources.*

Books

There are several colourful and accessible books about the Aztecs for children. You could try: The Aztecs, (Robert Nicholson, Two-Can JUMP! History, 1991); The Aztecs (Peter Hicks, Wayland, 1993); The Aztecs (Jacqueline Dineen, Heinemann, 1992); and The Aztecs (Tim Wood, Hamlyn, 1992). Robert Nicholson's book includes a photograph of the real Montezuma's head-dress.

Daily Life

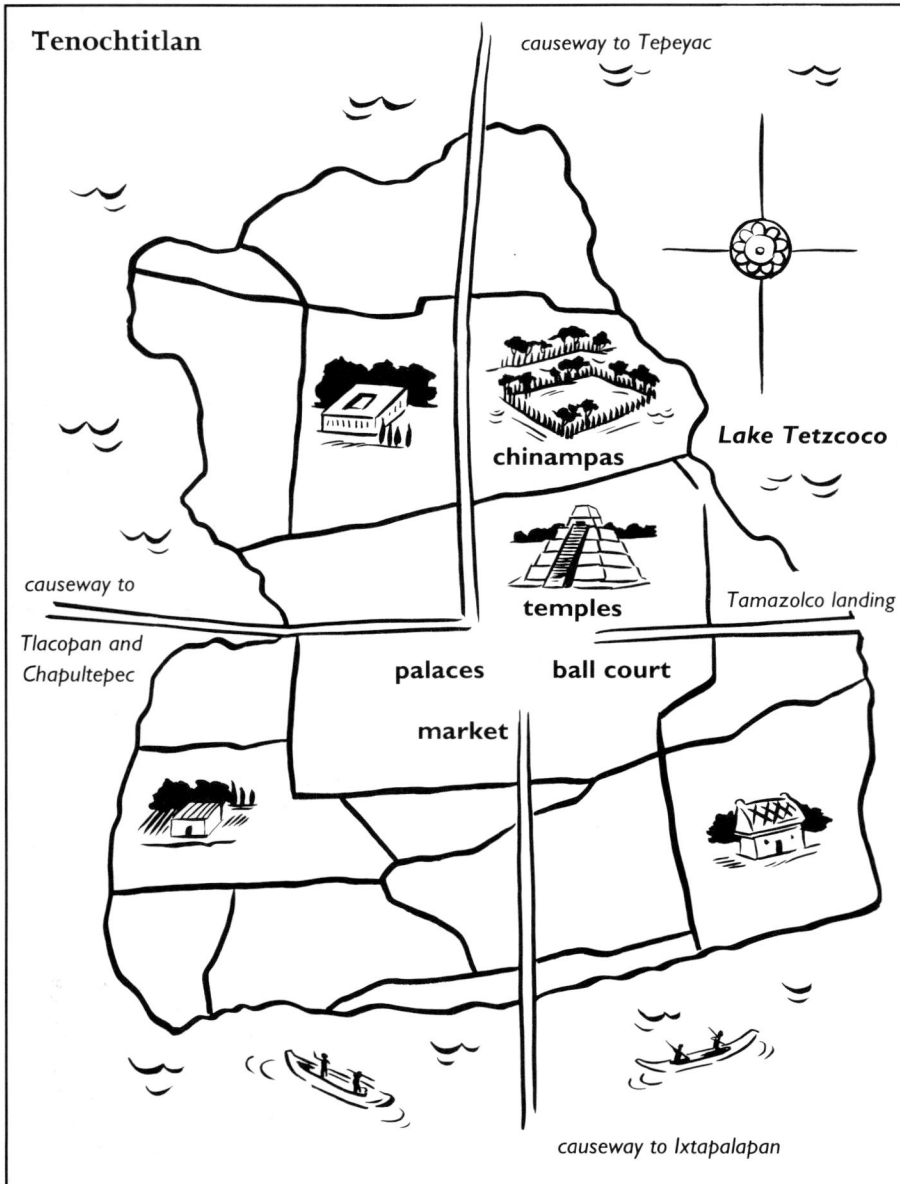

'The city of Tenochtitlan has large and beautiful squares where every article in use among the people is offered for sale. The main square is about three times the size of the square in Salamanca. Every day about twenty to twenty-five thousand people are there buying and selling. On market day, which is held every five days, there are forty to fifty thousand people.'

Tenochtitlan

causeway to Tepeyac

chinampas

Lake Tetzcoco

temples

Tamazolco landing

causeway to
Tlacopan and
Chapultepec

palaces   ball court

market

causeway to Ixtapalapan

The island city

Exploring life in the city of Tenochtitlan ties in well with the Geography Curriculum, in particular AT 4, the relationship between land use and settlement patterns. What were the practical problems of living in the middle of a lake. How did people get about? What did they eat? Were there any advantages to living on a lake?

At the centre of the island city was the main district, with several great temples and palaces, as well as a market-place, where goods from all over Mexico were sold. Spreading out from this centre was a regular network of paths and canals, which connected other districts of the city where tradespeople and farmers lived. Rich people lived in two-storey stone houses, while poorer people lived in small thatched huts near their fields. To get around the lake, the Aztecs used dug-out canoes.

Aztec daily life is a fascinating subject, not least because of the amazing city where the Aztecs lived. Tenochtitlan was built on marshy islands in the middle of a lake, and was joined to the shore by artificial stone causeways and an aqueduct which brought fresh water to the city. In 1519, it was one of the biggest cities in the world, around 7 km long from north to south. The Spaniards were amazed at its beauty. Yet it was built without the wheel, draught animals or iron tools, technological developments that were all taken for granted in the old world.

Fortunately, the Spaniards left several descriptions of life in Tenochtitlan when they first saw the city. This description of the market-place comes from a useful source entitled *The Chronicle of the Anonymous Conquistador*:

Farming and food

The food and farming methods of the Aztecs show how they had adapted to living on and around a shallow lake. The lake itself was rich in fish and waterbirds, which were hunted from canoes. The Aztecs also took other food items from the lake, which would not seem so appetizing to us. These included tadpoles, insect eggs and larvae!

The basic food, however, was maize, grown in fields reclaimed from the lake, called chinampas. These were small, artificial islands, which the Aztecs made by scooping mud from the lake bottom and piling it onto a base of wooden stakes and matted vegetation. Trees were planted around the edges to anchor the soil.

Each morning, Aztec women would grind the maize into flour using a stone rolling-pin. It was mixed with water and baked into tortillas on a flat stone over a fire. The tortillas were eaten with beans, tomatoes and chilli peppers. Mexican women still make tortillas in this way today.

People also kept turkeys and small hairless dogs, fattened and eaten on special occasions. Another Aztec delicacy was chocolate, made from the beans of a tree that grew in the rainforest. However, only rich people could afford to drink chocolate. The cacao beans from which it was made were also used as money!

Defence

One big advantage of living on an island was that Tenochtitlan was very easy to defend. It would have been difficult to attack by water, and the three stone causeways that linked the island to the lake shore all had gaps at regular intervals. Normally, these gaps were bridged by simple wooden planks, but the bridges could be withrawn quickly and easily if invaders approached.

Society

The Spaniards were amazed at how well-ordered and law-abiding Aztec society was. Everybody seemed to know his or her place, and crime was almost unknown. Children were taught to be obedient and to respect their elders. However, punishments could be very strict; there is a famous Aztec illustration showing a naughty child being held over a fire of smoking chilli peppers!

If you were an Aztec, you could also tell at a glance what sort of person another Aztec was. Social class was shown by the clothes you wore. The higher up your position, the finer your clothes and jewellery – wealthy and important people wore gold nose and lip plugs and fine feathers.

Activity
Using the map on the opposite page as a guide to the city layout, draw a large plan or frieze of Tenochtitlan. Try to illustrate and label all the following: pyramid-shaped temples and stone palaces at the centre; a market-place where items from all over Mexico were sold; a network of canals for transport with dug-out canoes going from place to place; the small thatched huts of ordinary people; maize fields and chinampas on the edges of the city; the causeways joining the city to the mainland. You could also add extra scenes to this basic plan – perhaps a religious dance or sacrifice in progress, or the Aztec army setting off to war.

Assessment
Covers **AT 1, Level 4** *Describe different features of an historical period.* This visual display is a good way of gathering and arranging different pieces of information about Aztec life in Tenochtitlan.

Books
A number of books contain useful information about the daily life of the Aztecs and their capital city, including Insights: Aztecs (Fiona McDonald, Oxford University Press, 1992) and What do we know about the Aztecs? (Joanna Defrates and Rob Shone, Simon and Schuster, 1992). The Aztecs (Robert Nicholson, Two-Can JUMP! History, 1992) includes a photograph of a chinampa and a recipe for tlaxcallis, the Aztec name for tortillas.

Aztec Religion

Tlaloc

What did the gods do?

The Aztecs believed that their lives depended on the gods. The rain god provided water for the Aztecs' crops, while the war god gave them victories. At a deeper level, the Aztecs also believed that the gods kept the universe in existence: they thought that the universe had already been destroyed four times and that they lived under the 'fifth sun'. One day, this sun too would be destroyed and all life on earth would end.

The Aztecs worshipped dozens of different gods. Their names are often long and difficult to pronounce, but you can get round this barrier by translating them into English.

The most important of the Aztec gods was Huitzilopochtli, or Blue Hummingbird. He was the god of war, and special protector of the Aztec people. Among other gods were: Tezcatlipoca (Smoking Mirror), god of the night sky; Quetzalcoatl (Feathered Serpent), god of the wind and of learning; Xiuhtecuhtli (Turquoise Lord), god of fire; and Tlaloc, the god of rain and lightning. Tlaloc was a very ancient god, worshipped long before the time of the Aztecs – the original meaning of his name is lost.

The Aztecs drew pictures of these gods and made sculptures of them. Tlaloc always has goggle eyes and protruding teeth; Huitzilopochtli has a blue warrior suit and a magic fire serpent weapon; Tezcatlipoca has a magic mirror for a foot and Quetzalcoatl is often shown with a bird's beak.

The hollow days

The end of the Aztec year, in February, was a particularly dangerous time, when the world might easily come to an end. For five days, called the 'hollow days', people stayed indoors. They let their fires go out and destroyed their furniture. Children were marched up and down to keep them awake – if they fell asleep, they might well turn into rats!

Activity
Aztec gods and priests make ideal subjects for artwork. Children could draw and paint the different gods, or make models of them, and then label them. Try to imagine what the priests, with their strange features, must have looked like. This artwork will make a striking classroom display.

Assessment
Covers **AT 3, Level I** *Communicate information acquired from an historical source.*

Quetzalcoatl

Priests

Throughout the year, a variety of complicated ceremonies had to be performed to win the favour of the gods and keep away disasters. The ceremonies included music, dancing and offerings to the gods. The Aztec priests were there to make sure that the right ceremonies were performed. They fasted, prayed and stuck thorns in their own flesh to summon visions of the gods and to look into the future.

Aztec priests were startling to look at. They mutilated their ears, filed their teeth into points and painted their bodies black with paint made from crushed beetles.

Tezcatlipoca

Sacrifice

The Aztecs thought that their gods needed to be fed in order to stay strong. If they were not fed, they would lose their power and the 'fifth sun' would be destroyed. The Aztecs offered food, such as maize cakes, to the gods, but the most precious food of all was human blood.

Huitzilopochtli

The Aztecs regularly drew their own blood with cactus spines and offered it to the god. They also offered the blood of prisoners, captured in battle. The prisoners were led up the steps of the great temple and then sacrificed. Their hearts were cut out and burned in braziers in front of statues of the gods. We know that some captives went willingly to their deaths, though others had to be drugged.

The ball game

The temple area in Tenochtitlan also held a ball court, where a ritual ball game was played. It was rather like basketball – the players had to hit a rubber ball through a ring. However, they were allowed to use only their hips, knees and elbows. The game had a religious significance. The results were used by the Aztec priests to predict the future.

Discussion

The Aztecs had many stories and legends about the gods and you could read one with your class. The Aztecs (Robert Nicholson, Two-Can JUMP! History, 1991) includes an Aztec story of how humans first began to grow maize, thanks to the help of the god, Quetzalcoatl. This story is a good way of showing the children the Aztec view that their lives were dependent upon the actions of the gods. What words can you think of to describe the feelings that the Aztecs might have had about their gods? Were they frightened by the power of the gods?

Assessment

Covers **AT 3, Level 3** *Make deductions from historical sources.* From discussing Aztec religious practices and listening to Aztec legends, have the children been able to develop an understanding of the relationship that existed between the Aztec people and their gods?

The Spaniards Arrive in Mexico

In the year 1518, messengers arrived in Tenochtitlan from the coast with amazing news. Two towers, or small mountains, had been seen floating on the water of the great sea. Strange people could be seen moving about on them. This was a Spanish expedition from Cuba, exploring the coast. After a brief visit, the ships sailed away.

The following year, the Spaniards came back in a fleet of eleven ships commanded by Hernan Cortes. The Aztecs sent messengers to the coast to greet the strangers and find out more about them.

Activity

Try to devise and carry out activities that will get the children to see the encounter between the Spanish and the Aztecs from both sides.

First, the children could pretend to be the Aztec messengers, sent to meet the Spaniards. They have to report on what they have seen to Montezuma. The Aztec ruler wants to find out what the strangers look like. Where do they come from? What things do they have with them? The messengers could write a report and draw what they have seen, or the children could act out a scene of the messengers reporting back to Montezuma.

Then try to see the encounter from the Spanish point of view. Ask the children to pretend to be one of Cortes' soldiers, writing a letter back home to Spain. The letter should describe everything that the soldier has seen in Tenochtitlan. What does he think is good about Aztec life? What does he dislike?

Assessment

Covers **AT 2, Level 2** *Show an awareness that different stories about the past can give different versions of what happened;* **AT 2, Level 3** *Distinguish between a fact and a point of view.* These activities help children to see historical events from more than one viewpoint. Use any written work that the children produce to begin a more general discussion about facts and points of view. Can the children understand the difference?

Books

A useful book for looking at the encounter between Spanish and Aztecs is Spaniards and the Aztecs: Face to Face (Fiona McDonald, Simon and Schuster, 1992). If you want to do more detailed research yourself, it is possible to read two fascinating and gripping accounts of the Spanish conquest, each written from a different perspective. The Aztec story of the conquest is contained in The Broken Spears: The Aztec Account of the Conquest of Mexico (edited by Miguel Leon-Portilla, Beacon Press, Boston, 1992). The Spanish side of events is contained in histories written by Cortes' own men, including The Conquest of New Spain (Bernal Diaz, Penguin Classics).

The meeting

The encounter between the Spaniards and the Aztecs is well documented, from an Aztec as well as from a Spanish point of view. Cortes and four of his men wrote about what they saw. The Aztecs also recorded their past, in picture histories and in stories which were memorized and passed on from the old to the young. In the later half of the sixteenth century, many of the Aztec stories about the coming of the Spaniards were written down by Spanish friars. Here is a typical extract from the Aztec history of the conquest. It is a description of the Spaniards given to Montezuma by the first Aztecs to see them:

'Their deer carry them on their backs wherever they wish to go. These deer are as tall as the roof of a house. The strangers' bodies are completely covered, so that only their faces can be seen. Their skin is white, as if it were made of lime. They have yellow hair, though some have black. Their hair is curly with very fine strands.'

The Spanish view

The Spaniards saw the encounter in a very different way.

They were amazed and delighted to learn of the wealth of the Aztecs, who gave them beautiful gifts. Mexico was clearly much richer than any of the Caribbean islands. However, they were also horrified by Mexican religion and the practice of human sacrifice. From their Christian point of view, they thought Aztec religion was devil worship. They believed that it was their duty to stamp it out and preach the 'true faith'. They were convinced that God would help them to convert the Aztecs.

Cortes was a bold, ambitious, and clever leader who quickly began to plan the conquest of Mexico. He was delighted to find that many of the peoples of Mexico had to pay tribute to the Aztecs and hated their overlords. In a letter to the King of Spain, Cortes wrote:

'When I saw the hatred between these peoples, I was greatly pleased, for it seemed to further my purpose considerably; as a consequence I might be able to subdue them more quickly, for, as the saying goes, 'divided they fall'. So I manoeuvred one against the other and thanked each side for their warnings and told each that I held his friendship to be of more worth than the others.'

23

The Spanish Conquest

Cross-Curricular Links:
Geography AT 1 Geographical skills
English AT 2 Reading

The Spanish conquest of Mexico, between 1519 and 1521, has all the elements of a gripping adventure story. Leaving Cuba with a fleet of 11 ships and 600 men, Cortes landed on the Mexican coast. After defeating the local chieftains in a skirmish, Cortes sailed along the coast, where he met Aztec tax gatherers and two ambassadors, sent by Montezuma from Tenochtitlan with valuable presents of gold.

Shortly after the visit of these ambassadors, the Spanish governor of Cuba sent instructions for Cortes to return to the island, but Cortes disobeyed these orders and decided to press on to the Aztec capital. He built a fortress on the coast and sank his own ships to stop any of his men from fleeing back to Cuba. The small Spanish force then set off for the heart of the Aztec Empire.

The march to Tenochtitlan

As the Spaniards marched inland, they met and fought a number of the different peoples who lived in Mexico. First Cortes defeated the Tlaxcalans, a fierce people who had remained independent of the Aztecs; then the Spanish troops entered the city of Cholulla, which was allied to the Aztecs. The Tlaxcalans told Cortes that he would be ambushed in Cholulla; no one knows if this was really true, but the Spaniards believed it and they attacked the Cholullans first, killing many of them. They then marched on to Tenochtitlan, accompanied by two thousand Tlaxcalans who had formed a pact against the Aztecs with Cortes.

When Montezuma heard of the Cortes' victories, he became very worried, and rather than attacking the Spaniards, he decided to welcome them into Tenochtitlan as guests. Cortes and his men were entertained as great chieftains, and were shown about the city, though Cortes remained suspicious of the Aztecs and thought they might try to ambush him again.

After two tense weeks, Cortes and his captains asked for an audience with Montezuma, seized him without warning, and took him back to their quarters. Montezuma was so shocked that he pretended to go and live in the Spanish encampment of his own free will.

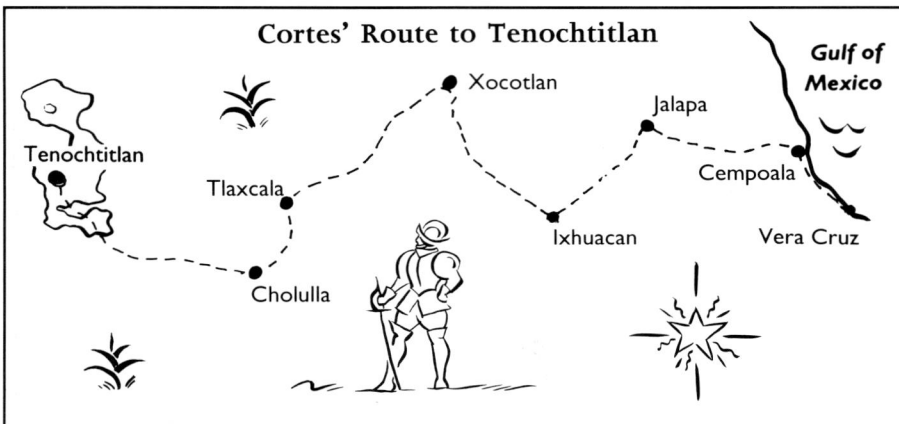

Cortes' Route to Tenochtitlan

Tenochtitlan • Tlaxcala • Cholulla • Xocotlan • Ixhuacan • Jalapa • Cempoala • Vera Cruz

Gulf of Mexico

Discussion

After going through the story of Cortes' conquest of Tenochtitlan, talk about all the reasons why he was successful. Children could make a list of these reasons – either individually, as a class or in groups, depending on how confident they are with handling the material.

Assessment

Covers **AT 1, Level 3b** *Give reasons for an historical event;* **AT 1, Level 4b** *Show an awareness that historical events usually have more than one cause and consequence;* **AT 1, Level 5c** *Show how different features in an historical situation relate to each other.* Discussing the reasons for the conquest of the Aztec Empire introduces children to a fairly complex sequence of causes and effects. It is important for children to try and understand how the various elements in the story fit together. More able children will be able to grasp that events may happen because a number of different causal factors combine in a particular way. (For instance, even with his superior weaponry, Cortes probably would not have defeated the Aztecs without the help of other Native American groups.)

Books

The Expedition of Cortes (Nigel Hunter, Wayland, 1990) tells the story of the Spanish invasion and conquest of Mexico. A number of the general children's books on the Aztecs also give accounts of the overthrow of Aztec power.

The defeat of the Aztecs

For a number of months, Cortes was virtually able to rule the city through Montezuma, but the Aztec warriors gradually became more and more restless. When the Spaniards massacred a large number of Aztecs during a religious ceremony, the warriors had finally had enough. They chose a new ruler and rose up against the Spaniards and Tlaxcalans, who were forced to flee from Tenochtitlan. Many Spaniards died during the retreat, which became known as the Noche Triste, or sad night.

Cortes had to spend time building up a new army, but in 1521, he returned with reinforcements from Cuba and laid siege to the Aztec capital. He was joined by many local peoples, who were eager to take part in the overthrow of the hated Aztecs. In the city of Tenochtitlan there was a terrible smallpox epidemic, and, with their water and food supplies cut off, the Aztecs were finally conquered.

Activity
Worksheet 4 is a diary of Cortes' journey from his landing in Mexico to his arrival in Tenochtitlan. Using the information on the worksheet, children should draw in the route on the map.

Assessment
Covers **AT 3, Level 3** *Make deductions from historical sources*. This is a reasonably straightforward exercise in extracting information from an historical source. It also practises children's map-work skills and devlops their ability to place events in chronological order.

How did Cortes defeat the Aztecs?

It seems astonishing that, with his tiny army, Cortes could have conquered a city of over 250,000 people. There were a number of different reasons for his success.

● One obvious reason is that the Spaniards had better technology. They used steel weapons, gunpowder and horses, while the Aztecs had only foot soldiers armed with flint weapons.

● The Spanish also fought in a different way from the Aztecs. The European troops were highly disciplined, and fought as a team, usually in a tight formation. They also fought to kill their enemies. The Aztec warriors, on the other hand, tended to fight much more as individuals, and they tried to capture prisoners (who would later be sacrificed to the gods) rather than killing the Spaniards straight out.

● A very important reason for Cortes' success was the help he received from his allies. As time went by, it became obvious that the Aztec tribute was hated by many of the other Mexican peoples, who joined Cortes' seige of Tenochtitlan.

● Some people think that Montezuma's actions contributed to the Aztecs' defeat. Why did he let Cortes into Tenochtitlan in the first place? Why did he allow himself to be taken prisoner? Some historians have suggested that Montezuma believed that Cortes was a god, and was afraid of him. Certainly, the Spanish must have seemed to possess almost supernatural powers, and Montezuma was confused by the way that the Europeans had such different forms of behaviour from the Aztecs.

● In the long run, the deadliest weapon that the Spaniards brought with them was disease. The Native Americans had no immunity to many common European diseases, and within just a couple of years of Cortes' arrival, many thousands of the Aztecs had already died of smallpox.

Legacy of the Conquest

When Columbus set out on his first voyage, he wanted to bring back gold for Spain and spread Christianity. Although he did not live to see it, both of these aims were fulfilled. Spain grew rich from the gold and silver of the Americas and the Catholic religion was established in all the lands conquered by the Spaniards.

However, there were many other consequences of the Spanish conquest, none of which had been foreseen by anyone. The biggest effect was the spread of European diseases in the 'New World'.

In the early sixteenth century, millions of Native Americans died of common illnesses such as small-pox, measles and influenza. They had no natural resistance to these diseases. The native population of Mexico fell from around 20 million in 1519 to under one million in 1600. The Tainos of Hispaniola and Cuba were completely wiped out. One eyewitness wrote that the Native Americans seemed to die almost as soon as they came into contact with a Spaniard.

The destruction of the old civilizations

Besides the damage wreaked by European disease, the Spaniards consciously did everything possible to destroy the old ways of life, burning books and destroying temples. In their place, they built churches and set up crosses. Anyone who still worshipped the old gods could be burned at the stake. Native American works of art were melted down for the gold and silver they contained.

Many of the native peoples were enslaved by the Europeans, and forced to work in gold and

Discussion
Your class should try to see the results of the conquest from both the Spanish and the Aztec point of view. You could read out and discuss these two extracts. The first is an Aztec account of the seige of Tenochtitlan:

'The Spanish blockade caused great anguish in the city. The people were tormented by hunger and many starved to death. There was no fresh water. People roasted whatever they could find and then ate it. They ate the bitterest weeds and even dirt. Nothing can compare with the horrors of that siege and the agonies of the starving.'

The second extract is a more general description by a Spaniard of the conquest of the Mexico:

'The conquest of Mexico and the conversion of the native peoples was a great event. Many powerful kingdoms were conquered with little bloodshed or harm to the inhabitants. Many millions were baptized and now live, thanks be to God, as Christians. Men gave up their many wives and took one alone. They cast down their many different idols and believed in Our Lord God. And they abandoned the sacrifice of living men and learned to hate the practice of eating of human flesh.'

Assessment
Covers **AT 2, Level 2** *Show an awareness that different stories about the past can give different versions of what happened.* **AT 2, Level 3** *Distinguish between a fact and a point of view.* Can the children tell which writer was unhappy about the conquest, and which thought that it was a good thing? Ask them to think closely about the language of the two extracts. Which words show us what the writers really felt? (The Aztec account has words like 'anguish', 'tormented' and 'horrors'.) Which parts of the story does the Spanish writer leave out and are any parts of his account actually incorrect?

silver mines, or on the large Spanish farms and plantations. Native Americans were even made to dress differently, in trousers instead of loincloths and cloaks. They were taught that their own way of life was bad, and that everything European was better.

The destruction of the native civilizations by the Europeans seems quite scandalous to us today, but at the time, most Spaniards did not think that they were doing anything wrong. They believed that their actions were justified because they were bringing Christianity to the Native People. They banned human sacrifice and ended the constant warfare that had been a feature of Aztec life. Working in a Spanish silver mine was a small price for an Aztec warrior to pay

Activity

A good way of rounding off this study unit is to find out about life in Mexico today. Gather information from library books and other sources such as travel brochures. Which parts of Mexican life come from Spain? Which go back to the Aztecs? You could look at religion, food and language. Some Mexican festivals, such as the Day of the Dead, are a mixture of both Spanish and Aztec cultures.

Assessment

Covers **AT I, Level 4a** *Recognize that over time some things changed and other things stayed the same.*

Books

Useful information books about Mexico include: We Live in Mexico (C. Somonte, Wayland, 1984); World in View: Mexico (Amanda Hopkinson, Heinemann, 1991); Mexico is My Country (B and C Moon, Wayland, 1986).

for being turned away from devil worship and having his soul saved.

There were some Spaniards, however, who questioned the results of the conquest. Pedro de Cieza de Leon, criticized the behaviour of his countrymen:

'It is no small sorrow to reflect that we Christians have destroyed so many kingdoms. For wherever Christians have passed, conquering and discovering, it seems as though a fire has gone, eating up everything.'

The wealth of the New World

The arrival of the Spanish changed life in the Americas for ever, yet it also had many effects on life in Europe too. An enormous number of the plants and animals that we use every day were unknown in Europe before Columbus's voyage to the New World. Potatoes, tomatoes, chilli peppers, maize, kidney beans, turkeys, chocolate, tobacco and rubber all come from the Americas. You could bring a few of these items into your class, and ask the children to think of all the foodstuffs made from maize or potatoes. Can they imagine life without chips or cornflakes?

America also received many new kinds of food from Europe: wheat and sugar cane, as well as new kinds of cattle, sheep and pigs. Just as important was the new technology – the Europeans brought iron and steel tools, and wheeled transport pulled by horses and donkeys.

❶ Europe Before Columbus

name ....

This map of the world was drawn before Columbus's voyage. Compare it with a modern map.

❓ Which countries are the right shape?

❓ Which countries are the wrong shape?

❓ Which countries are missing?

Try to fit the labels to the map.

Britain	France	Spain
Italy	Africa	Russia
India	China	Sri Lanka

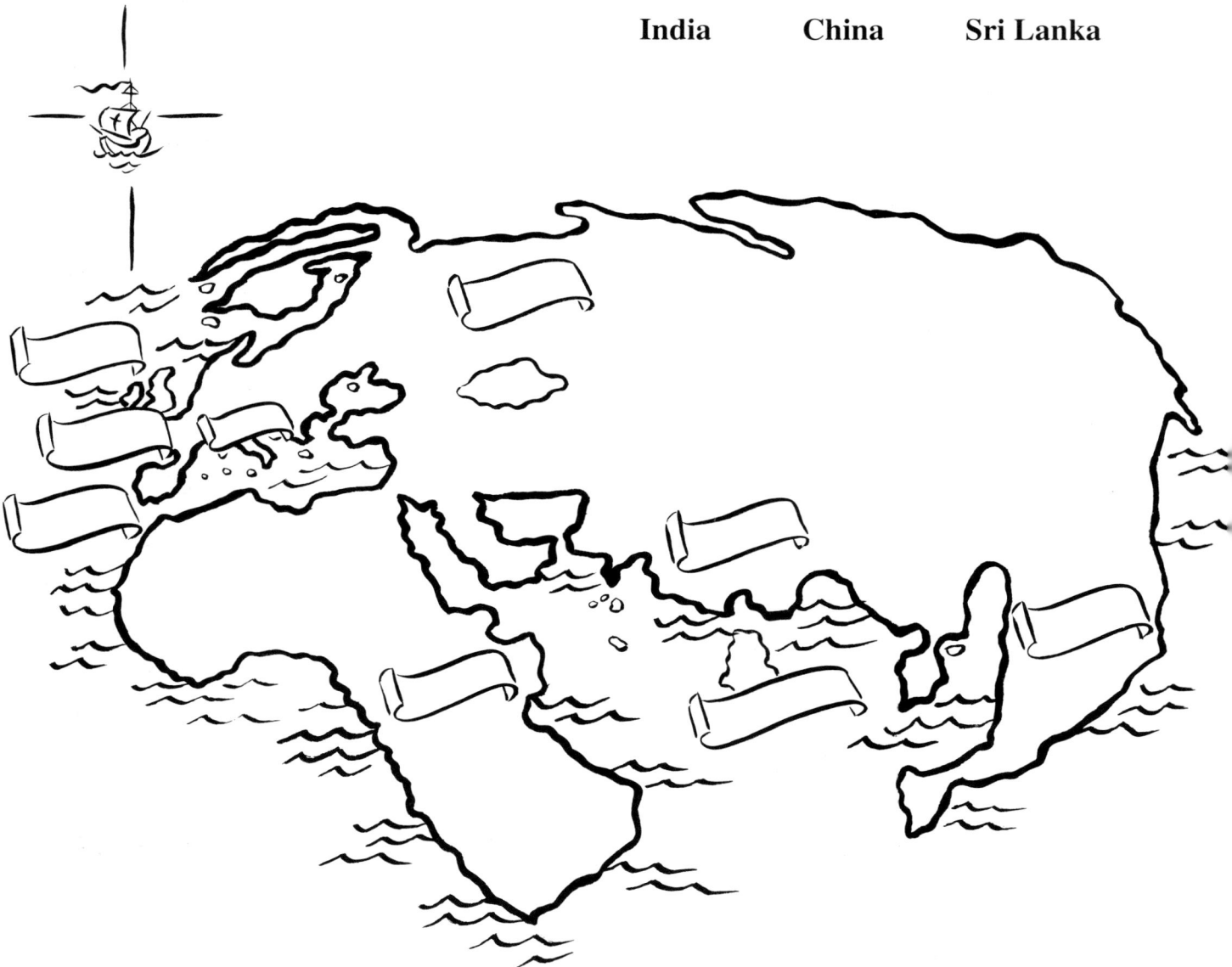

❷ Columbus's Voyage Across the Atlantic, 1492

name ....

3 August	The Santa Maria, the Pinta and the Nina set sail from Spain.
9 August	The Pinta's rudder keeps breaking, so the ships call in at the Canary Islands for repairs.
6 September	The ships leave the Canary Islands, but there is little wind.
8 September	A strong wind blows from the north-east. The ships sail well, with a good wind behind them.
17 September	Seaweed is seen floating on the sea, so the sailors think that land is near. Many dolphins appear, and the crew of the Nina manages to kill one.
18 September	The wind still blows the ships to the west. The sailors worry how they will ever find a wind to blow them back home again.
23 September	The sea is calm and smooth. The crew grumbles about the lack of wind.
10 October	The sailors complain about the length of the voyage but Columbus says that he will not turn back until he has found land.
11 October	Floating twigs are seen, a sure sign that land is near. The crew is relieved. One sailor shouts out that he has seen land and soon everyone can see a small island nearby.

❸ *An Aztec Tribute List* name ....

The Aztecs forced the peoples they conquered to give them valuable goods, called tribute. They kept records of the tribute using picture writing. This is how they showed some of the goods:

*A bunch
of feathers*

*A bag of
cacao beans*

*A mask of jade
(jade is a green-
coloured precious stone)*

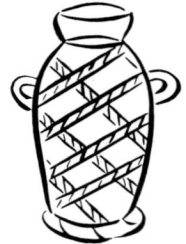

*A jar
of honey*

Amounts were shown by using dots and flags.

Each dot ● stands for <u>one</u>. Each flag ⊏ stands for <u>twenty</u>.

*This is how the
Aztecs showed 40
bags of cacao beans.*

*This picture
means 23
jade masks.*

❓ What do the pictures below mean? Write the answers underneath.

....

❓ Can you draw Aztec picture writing for these pieces of tribute:

| 3 masks
of jade | 27 jars
of honey | 63 bags
of cacao beans | 8 bunches
of feathers |
|---|---|---|---|
| | | | |

❹ Cortes' March to Tenochtitlan

name ....

This is the story of Cortes' march to Tenochtitlan in 1519.
Can you plot his route on the map?

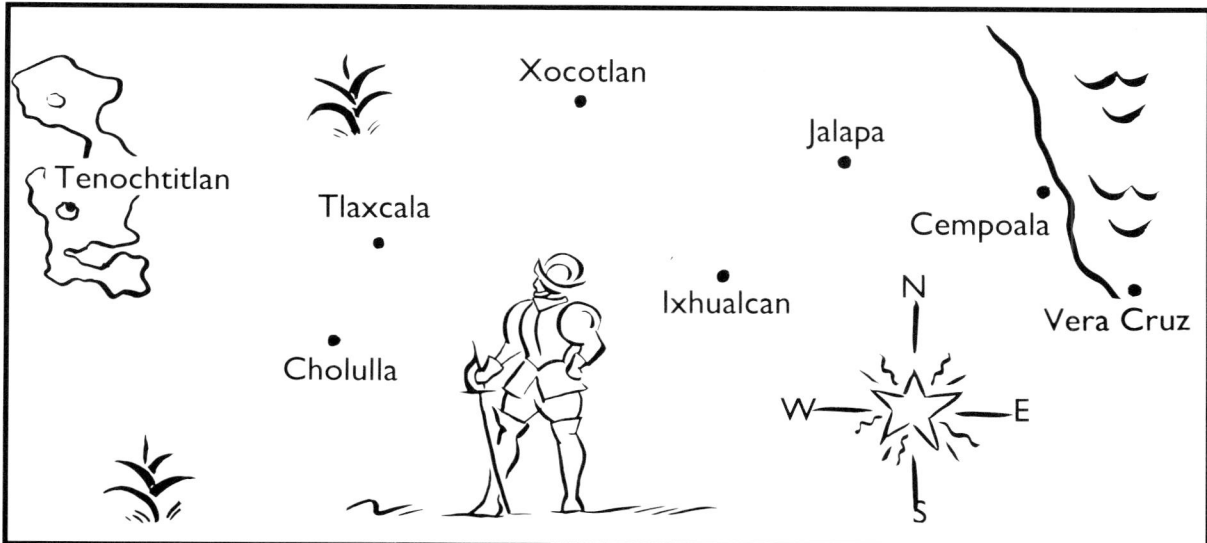

April	The Spaniards land on the coast, at Cempoala.
May – July	They build a town on the coast called Vera Cruz.
August	They set off inland, north-west to Jalapa. From Jalapa, they travel south-west through steep mountains to Ixhuacan. Then they cross a desert to Xocotlan.
August – September	The Spaniards go south-west to Tlaxcala. The Tlaxcalans attack them but cannot beat the European soldiers. They offer to become the Spaniards' friends and help them against the Aztecs.
October	The Spaniards and Tlaxcalans travel south-west, to Cholulla. The Tlaxcalans tell the Spaniards that the Cholullans plan to attack. The Spaniards attack first, killing many Cholullans.
November	Cortes and his men travel north-west, to Tenochtitlan. They reach the Aztec city on 8 November 1519.

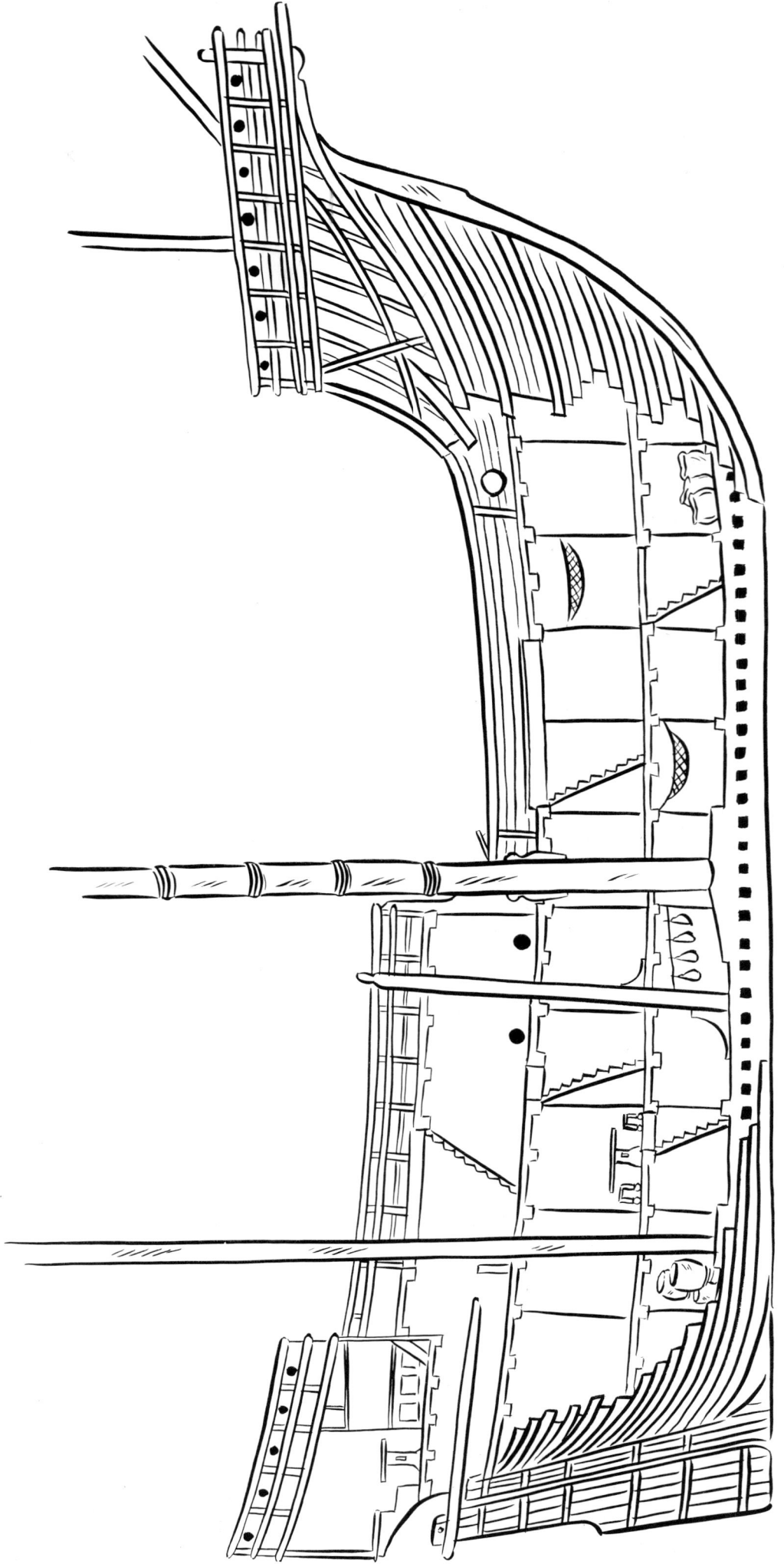

5 *Life on Board the Santa Maria*

name ....